Peter Rabbit
Playtime Activity
Sticker Book

FREDERICK WARNE

Who Are They Afraid Of?

Find the missing stickers, then name the different characters or animals. Who is afraid of who? Follow the lines to find out.

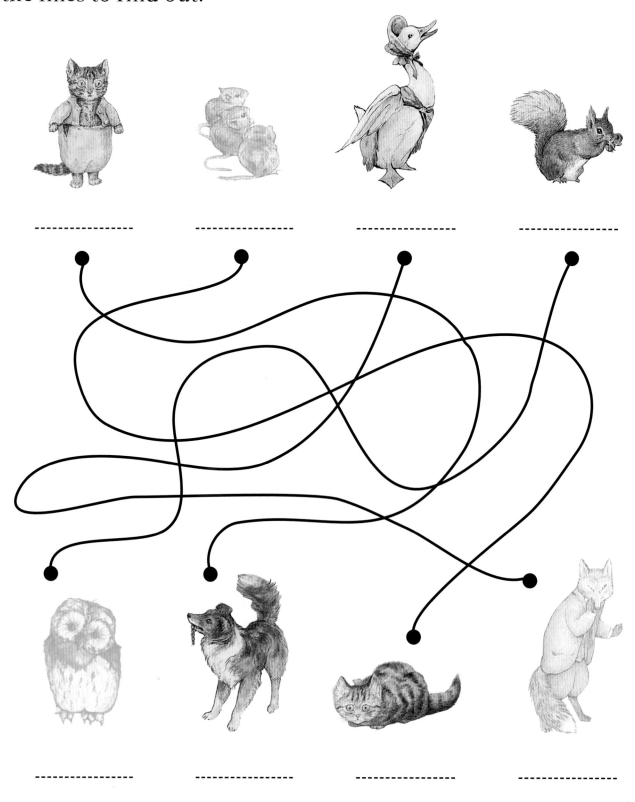

----------------- ----------------- ----------------- -----------------

----------------- ----------------- ----------------- -----------------

Cats Under the Covers

Tom Kitten and his sisters were *very* naughty indeed! Can you colour the picture?

Tom Kitten's Lucky Escape

Tom has an adventure when he discovers the secret hideout of the rats, Samuel Whiskers and Anna Maria. Play this game to see who can help Tom escape the fastest. Find stickers to tell the story before you begin.

There's a sticker for the winner too!

1 START	2	3
16	15 Tom is tied up. Go back 3 spaces.	14
17	18	19
32	31	30
33	34	35 Samuel doesn't want Tom. Move ahead 1 s
48 FINISH	47	46

This is a game for 2-4 players. You will need: a button or coin for each player and a dice. Roll the dice to move your counter around the board. The winner is the first to finish!

	5	6	7	8
falls down a hole. Miss a turn.		Tom finds a hiding spot! Move ahead to number 10.		
	12	11	10	9
	21	22	23	24 Mrs. Tabitha looks for Tom. Move ahead 2 spaces.
	28 Tom is rolled in pastry. Go back 2 spaces.	27	26	25
	37	38	39 Samuel and Anna Maria run away. Move to 42.	40
	44 Tom has to have a hot bath. Move back 2 spaces.	43	42	41

Count Up!

Ginger and Pickles run a very busy shop.
Anyone who is anyone shops here. Look at the picture
below and count how many of each animal there are.
Find the correct number sticker for each box.

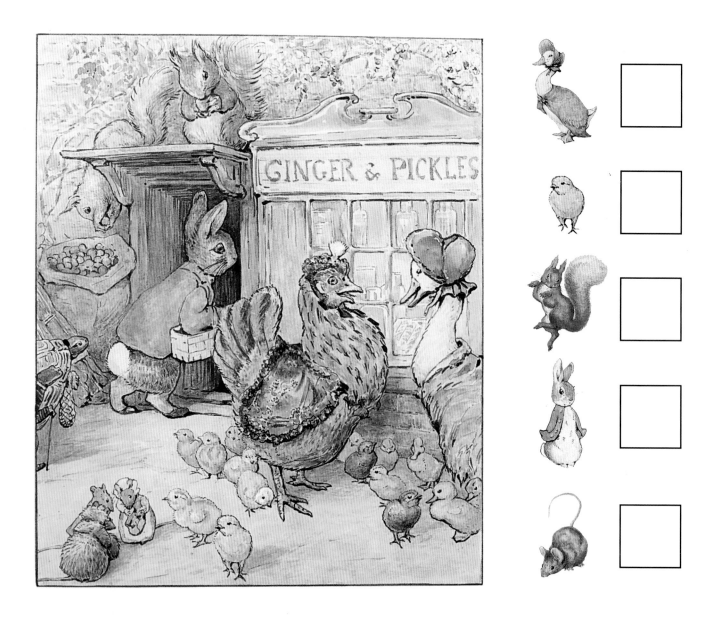

What else can you see in the picture? _ _ _ _ _ _ _ _ _ _ _ _ _ _ _ _ _ _ _

Blackberries For Tea

Flopsy, Mopsy and Cotton-tail, who were good little bunnies, went down the lane to gather blackberries. Can you find the sticker, then colour the picture?

Guess Who?

Peter Rabbit has lots of adventures and meets lots of new friends. Which creatures do the shadows below belong to? Find the stickers to match, and write their names underneath.

Who is your favourite? ----------------------

pages 4-5

page 2

pages 4-5

page 10

page 8

1 15

3 2

1

page 6

page 12

page 7

W

E

L

D N

L O E

page 7

page 8

Wrap Up Warm

Peter Rabbit, Flopsy, Mopsy and Cotton-tail are getting ready to go out. Colour the picture.

A Handsome Gentleman

Colour this picture
of Jemima chatting
to her handsome
gentleman friend.

Hide and Seek

Mr. McGregor is sure there are lots of naughty rabbits hiding in his garden. How many can you spot?

What other animal is in the garden with Mr. McGregor?

Benjamin's Crossword Puzzle

It looks as though Peter Rabbit and Benjamin Bunny are in Mr. McGregor's garden again. Use the clues to help you fill in the words. Find the missing stickers before you begin.

Clues

Across:
1. Peter and Benjamin hide themselves under this.
2. Peter Rabbit wraps himself up in this when his coat goes missing.
3. Peter Rabbit's mother uses these when she is cooking.
4. All rabbits like to eat this green vegetable!

Down:
1. It's in Mr. McGregor's .... that Peter gets into trouble.
2. This is the animal Peter and Benjamin hide from.
3. Mr. McGregor has a few of these growing in his garden.
4. This is the colour of Peter Rabbit's handkerchief.

Spot the Difference

Here are two pictures
of Mr. Jeremy Fisher
preparing to catch
some minnows for dinner.
See if you can find five
differences between the
pictures. Circle them in
the bottom picture.

Bunny Fun

Flopsy, Mopsy and Cotton-tail
are helping Mrs. Rabbit!
Colour in the picture below.

How many bottles can you count in the picture?   _____

Congratulations!

You've done a great job! To show their appreciation, Peter Rabbit and his friends have a special message for you. Find a sticker for the first letter of each picture to read it.

Answers

Page 2

Who Are They Afraid Of?

Tom Kitten is afraid of Kep the dog.
The mice are afraid of Miss Moppet.
Jemima Puddle-duck is afraid of the foxy
gentleman.
Squirrel Nutkin is afraid of Old Brown,
the owl.

Page 6

Count Up!

There are: 1 duck, 15 chicks, 2 squirrels,
1 rabbit and 3 mice.

Page 8

Guess Who?

Squirrel   Kitten

Duck   Butterfly

Rabbit   Dog

Page 11

Hide and Seek

There are 10 rabbits.

Page 12

Benjamin's Crossword Puzzle

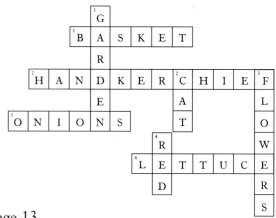

Page 13

Spot the Difference

Page 14

Bunny Fun

There are 2 bottles

Page 15

Congratulations!

The message says: WELL DONE